Shrinking Bones

Judy K. Mosher

A Publication of The Poetry Box®

©2018 Judy K. Mosher
All rights reserved.

Editing & Book Design by Shawn Aveningo Sanders
Cover Design by Robert R. Sanders
Author Photo by Marylou Butler

No part of this book may be reproduced in any matter whatsoever without permission from the author, except in the case of brief quotations embodied in critical essays, reviews and articles.

ISBN: 978-1-948461-10-8
Printed in the United States of America.

Published by The Poetry Box®, 2018
Beaverton, Oregon
ThePoetryBox.com

In Memory of Mi Mamacita
Lynn (Olsen) Mosher
1926 - 2015

Contents

Shrinking	7
Remembering Red Bear	9
The Back Forty	11
Fragile Fingers	13
Seventy Year Awakening	15
Red Scissors	17
Chatter	19
Loving Mama	21
Mother's Eyes	23
The Big Empty	25
Spine	27
Acknowledgments	29
Praise for *Shrinking Bones*	31
About the Author	33
About The Poetry Box Chapbook Prize	35

HUMERUS, RADIUS, AND ULNA

| hu·mer·us |
| ra·di·us |
| ul·na |

the three long bones comprising the upper arm and the forearm; the bones and muscles of the arm enable humans to reach, push and pull

Shrinking

bones loom large beneath her sagging skin
arms that wrestled her world are now soft
no shopping, chopping, baking rhubarb
pie, resigned hands rest limp on her lap

she fears falling, sits humbly in her chair
robins, doves peer through the window
sing to her from the sunbaked birdbath
Solitude   her primary companion

Mother   shrinks   more each day
60 years, my arms stretched up
for her embrace   now I reach
down to hug her fragile frame

her impatience already died
in stillness, we await sunset
with twilight we yawn,
expect another dawn

sleep sidesteps me
mind dreads when

my wobbly world
shrinks for
good

BONE MARROW

| bon mar·ro |

found in the hollow cavity of long bones of the upper and lower extremities, this tissue is responsible for the creation and growth of blood cells which circulate all over the body

Remembering Red Bear

His black button eyes
gazed warmly at her
when she woke

in this new, blue bedroom.
Walls changed like chameleons
often during those years

of the Great Depression.
A Norwegian immigrant,
her Papa seldom had rent money.

Handyman services fed the
family but by month end
failed to cover the rent

so like gypsies they moved
their pots, pans, paint brushes
in the still of the night.

For my Mother, change lodged
deep, the absolute
marrow of her bones

for her parents ensured
her red stuffed bear
awoke beside her, always.

LEGS

| legs |

the femur, tibia and fibula are the bones of the lower extremity working collectively to support the skeleton's upright position and to engage powerful muscles to propel mobility

The Back Forty

In her final years
we plant a vegetable garden in her back yard.

Besides watching flickers, spotted towhees
she measures her summer days
by the length of the zucchini.

She affectionately calls the 6' by 8' raised-bed
the back forty. Her task is to turn the spigot
rotating her and the drip irrigation.

When the trek to that spigot
is too much for weary legs
she sits with her old friends — table and chair

together they gaze at fat robins splashing
and tomatoes too stubborn
to ever turn red.

FINGER

| fin·ger |

any of the five digits of the hands of primates; each finger ordinarily has 2 to 3 segments

Fragile Fingers

With age, my fragile mother disappears
into a teacup version of her precious photograph,
while I long to return to misty times of
laughter, lilacs, and Liberace.

My mind sees her slicing peaches, flour-brushed
fingers curious to create a new dish.
Who is this impostor, with
Einstein-fluffed white hair?

I peer deep into Mother's mirror
see there my own fragile future of
soft suspenders that hold but cannot heal.
I escape south to the Bosque

ride the wind with snow geese,
sandhill cranes, red-tailed hawks —
their existence as precarious as ours,
their feathers less porous to the rain.

HYOID (OR HYOID BONE)

| hy·oid bone |

a U-shaped bone in the throat; at the base of the tongue, essential to breathing, swallowing, and speaking

Seventy Year Awakening

Mother told me
her mother was Rosie the Riveter.
She would rivet, drill, weld, meld
metal into weapons of war
with patriotic pride same
as baking apple pie.

Mother told me
youth were wrong about Vietnam.
A knife sliced our nation in two;
generations severed, families divided.
Street protests, tear gas, flights to Canada
shook the chaff from the grain.

After 2001, Mother was stunned
as patriotic young men, women
enlisted to don guns, combat boots,
fight terror in this war du jour.
Retaliation gets us nowhere,
Mother told me.

HAND

| hand |

twenty-seven bones join to form palm and fingers; provides complex functions of gesture, grasp, and holding

Red Scissors

Fragile fingers
squeeze the scissors,
papers cut precisely.

At eighty-seven, her scissors
always park themselves beside
her frayed maroon placemat.

She hides things there —
treasures clipped from magazines,
newspapers, even her mail.

Tidbits for conversation
smother under that placemat,
revive when visitors arrive.

Silver blades with red handles
in perfect reach
grasp for moments like this,

when the hope of the
winning lottery ticket
falls like spent confetti.

OSSICLES (OR AUDITORY OSSICLES)

| os·si·cles |

tiny, middle-ear bones (malleus, incus, and stapes) which transmit sound waves for hearing

Chatter

Chatter, squawk, honk
geese wake in the dark.
Chirp, screech, quack
quite a conversation.
Do they know sunrise
bursts in an hour, or
did they chatter all night?

My parents kept chatter
alive all night with
talk radio. Drove me
crazy as an adult home
for an overnight visit —
24-hour background sound.

Mom claimed it all began
when her Father was dying
of cancer. She couldn't sleep,
the radio distracted and
comforted. He passed.

At 87, her radio still chatters
all night, after she carefully
undresses her dentures
and hearing aide.

FOOT

| foot |

an extremely strong, complex structure of twenty-six bones, attaching to the lower leg, for the purpose of human mobility

Loving Mama

Who did I think I was supposed to love?
The boy who took my breath with his goodbye?
I look around, take off my fighting gloves
see weary frailty in Mother's eyes.

I glance away, distract to something new,
the patience gene is not one I imbue.

I kneel, lift her wrinkled foot in my hands
massage, then manicure her broken nails.
The wound upon her shin looks like quicksand
I re-dress and caress her as she pales.

Finally, I found gestures for her care
for all the times she bathed me, combed my hair.

ORBIT

| or·bit |

the specialized skull socket structured to cradle the eye and provide protection on three sides by seven bones of the cranium

Mother's Eyes

Mother died as she lived:
full up with fascination-observation.
Her tender-trusting eyes find mine

through the wooden screen door,
her body blending more with the
hospice bed than with those eyes.

Deep artist-observer eyes
like liquid they float sunken in their orbits,
still flutter like bees over blossoms.

"Don't let your coffee get cold" she prompts.
In her sphere I forget my cup on the table, more
desirous of drinking Mother's eyes, wise, musings

from quiet innocence she ponders her passing,
"Soon, I'll look back on this life like someone peers
through a window" her hands cup beside earnest eyes.

"Now, my soul plans its next adventure."
"Any hint of what that will be?" I want to know.
She shakes her head and with it shakes away thought.

Mother is now pure observation, and
of one thing I am sure
she walked into that valley,

eyes wide-open
observing, positioning herself
before her next blossom.

PHANTOM LIMB

| phan·tom limb |

the continued sensation after a limb has been amputated; pain or non-painful perception of presence where a limb no longer exists

The Big Empty

Sometimes I wonder,
how empty can be so full of feeling?
Like a phantom limb, I feel your presence.
It aches where you were.

Your footsteps echo through our home,
I see you sit in all your familiar places.
Your body brushes past mine
and I smell you on the pillow.

How could you disappear?
I still feel you here.
And my mind only half works —
did the other half go with you?

Yesterday someone asked about you.
Like a thermometer,
my mercury of memory
warmed me ten degrees, hearing your name aloud.

I lied and said it was getting easier.
How can I explain
the Big Empty has moved in
and I cannot wash the pillowcase?

SPINE

| spine |

the backbones, also called the vertebral column, which provide protection for the spinal cord

Spine

even knowing her fragility
shock shuffles a two-step across
my silent brain

even knowing her readiness
grief swamps   tangles me
in murky weeks   stalls momentum

even knowing her inevitable end
sorrow exhausts me, drums upon
my hundred-pound heart

even knowing I would bury her
the cardboard box of cremain dust
is   just   not   her

her silken thread spirals my DNA
her song vibrates my spine
her stories gesture my hands

but her presence   most unnerving
reflects in the mirror
each morning

Acknowledgments

With gratitude to the editors of the following publications where these poems first appeared:

"Fragile Fingers" and "Chatter" in *Bosque Rhythms*

"Seventy Year Awakening" in *Santa Fe Literary Review*

"The Big Empty" in *Adobe Walls*

❉ ❉ ❉

I cherish my circle of creative writers in Santa Fe, NM for their camaraderie, challenge, and affirmation. With healthy doses of laughter, we bolster each other on through the seriousness life deals to us. My special gratitude to Miriam Sagan, Cheryl Marita, Paula Miller, and Lib O'Brien who fanned life into this manuscript from its first ember.

With a grateful heart, I thank Marylou Butler and my given and chosen heart families. I am consistently blessed by your generosity and kindness.

Praise for *Shrinking Bones*

"In *Shrinking Bones* you come to know a mother and her daughter as Judy K. Mosher's mother ages, shrinks, and dwindles toward death. Mosher skillfully juxtaposes each poem with a description of bones – fingertips, ossicles, orbits, even a phantom limb – to build a framework of tender poems that detail how her mother cared for her, mellowed as time passed, even what made her mother laugh. Mosher's sensitive and delicate poetic touch shares how she tended her mother's wounds at the end of a long life and holds her memory now with each look in the mirror. If your relationship with your mother was not thus, you might wish it could have been."

~ Tricia Knoll, author of *How I Learned To Be White* and *Broadfork Farm*

"As the skeleton is the hardscape of the body, so poetry creates a precise armature of language on which to hang experience and emotion. Judy Mosher has done a masterful job of bringing anatomy and poetry together in a way that enhances the understanding of both. The metaphors here give the reader new insight into the universality — and specifics — of the mother-daughter bond. An enlightening collection!"

~ Miriam Sagan, poet

"To witness the death of her mother and her own grief, Mosher has invoked the metaphor of the bones of the body to describe the gentle path to the end. Her mastery, the metaphor and the simplicity of the poems focus a unique light on the journey."

~ Lee Firestone Dunne, author of *Life in the Poorhouse* and *Cocktail Shaker*

About the Author

Judy K Mosher, Ph.D., writes poetry and prose from her home in Santa Fe, where she wanders the mountains and arroyos with her golden retriever, Jessie. Home for over thirty years, New Mexico always kindles awe.

Judy's professional life primarily consisted of teaching in higher education. Her Ph.D. specialties were Biomechanics and Exercise Physiology. As a professor, she facilitated nursing, physical therapy, and physical education students' mastery of anatomy and physiology. Judy has also worked in academic, environmental, and community non-profit administration. She recently earned a Certificate in Creative Writing from Santa Fe Community College.

Many American adult children experience the challenges of distance when their parents age. Judy feels blessed that her Mother relocated making Santa Fe her home during her final twenty years. When poor health arrived, geographical convenience and a strong adult mother-daughter friendship provided a container until Evelyn passed at age eighty-eight. Their time together seeded the poems in this collection.

Her prose and poetry have been published in *Adobe Walls*, *CALYX*, *Malpais Review*, *Noyo River Review*, and *200newmexicopoems* among other places. She has received finalist and honorable mention awards in numerous poetry contests. Judy co-authored *Bosque Rhythms*, a collection of poems dedicated to Bosque del Apache Wildlife Refuge, with Lee Dunne, Cheryl Marita, Paula Miller and Elizabeth O'Brien. Bosque Rhythms was a 2015 Finalist in the New Mexico-Arizona Book Awards.

Shrinking Bones is her first chapbook.

Website: http://JudyKMosher.wordpress.com

About The Poetry Box Chapbook Prize

In 2018, The Poetry Box introduced their annual Chapbook Prize competition, awarding publication to at least one poet. The contest is open to both established poets and emerging talent alike, and the editors reserve the right to select more than one poet's manuscript for publication. Currently, the contest is open to poets residing in the United States and is open for submissions each year during the month of February.

2018 Winners

First Prize:
Shrinking Bones by Judy K. Mosher (NM)

Second Prize:
November Quilt by Penelope Scambly Schott (OR)

Third Prize (tie):
14: Antología del Sonoran by Christopher Bogart (NJ)
Fireweed by Gudrun Bortman (CA)

www.ingramcontent.com/pod-product-compliance
Lightning Source LLC
LaVergne TN
LVHW020501080526
838202LV00057B/6091